ARCHI-TOONS

For Valerie, Adelaide, Madeline and Julian. Thanks for the smiles.

Richard Bynum

Published in Great Britain in 2003 by Wiley-Academy, a division of John Wiley & Sons Ltd
Copyright © 2003   John Wiley & Sons Ltd, The Atrium, Southern Gate, Chichester,
                           West Sussex PO19 8SQ, England
                           Telephone   (+44) 1243 779777

Email (for orders and customer service enquiries): cs-books@wiley.co.uk
Visit our Home Page on www.wileyeurope.com or www.wiley.com

Other Wiley Editorial Offices
John Wiley & Sons Inc., 111 River Street, Hoboken, NJ 07030, USA
Jossey-Bass, 989 Market Street, San Francisco, CA 94103-1741, USA
Wiley-VCH Verlag GmbH, Boschstr. 12, D-69469 Weinheim, Germany
John Wiley & Sons Australia Ltd, 33 Park Road, Milton, Queensland 4064, Australia
John Wiley & Sons (Asia) Pte Ltd, 2 Clementi Loop #02-01, Jin Xing Distripark, Singapore 129809
John Wiley & Sons Canada Ltd, 22 Worcester Road, Etobicoke, Ontario, Canada M9W 1L1

ISBN 0470854065

Cover design: Artmedia Press Ltd, London
Text design: Liz Brown
Typeset by Atelier Data Services, St Austell, Cornwall, UK

Printed and bound in Italy

ARCHI-TOONS

Funniness, Comedy & Delight

Richard T. Bynum, Jr

WILEY-ACADEMY

INTRODUCTION

I am an architect. I don't remember why I chose this profession on career day in high school and I certainly had no idea what a wonderful adventure it would become. Maybe at the time it was an art job that seemed safe and dignified. Maybe it was that my dad had aspired to be the same but money and college didn't work out for him as he had planned. Maybe it was Mike Brady. Maybe it was my fort built above girl level in the cedar tree in my backyard. Or maybe it was because I thought I could make the world a better place by giving people better public and private environments in which to dwell, work and function. Maybe I don't remember... but one thing of which I am certain: I love what I do.

I love being an architect. I love all things architecture and architectural. I even love the study of the history of architecture but this long term infatuation is not to be confused with obsession. The simple fact is that the architect is academically instructed and professionally trained to be an observer of life. It is an attribute that can't be turned off once it is turned on; it can only be temporarily suppressed by sheer will power or medication.

I have chosen to channel my continuous live input of raw environmental data into a graphic exercise called Archi-toons. Cartooning, I have found, is not only therapeutic but can function as an effective method of communicating social commentary, cultural observation or just plain old funny stuff. Twenty years in the path and practice of the architectural profession, in large offices and small, have provided me with ample fodder of the plight, struggles, idiosyncrasies, and daily experiences of the architectural profession as well as the design and the construction industry.

Archi-toons was never conceived to be a running comic strip. Although the entertainers throughout the pages of *Archi-toons* are varied and at times eccentric, there are a few characters that are intertwined throughout these pages. The stereotypical professional, the academic role model, the public's perception of our craft and many icons of our industry are all "celebrated" in the broadest sense of the word.

The architectural office that contains the key players is known as Dezinefirm Inc. Founded eons ago as a three man start-up, the firm has evolved into a typical microcosm of the professional corporate world. Within this framework there are several individuals that will make you say "He is just like..." only the hair and clothes have changed (and hopefully the names too). For example, the principal of design at Dezinefirm Inc is known as McGlade. He has only one name but also one big ego. He is faithfully served by Zack, the Project Architect. You know the type. Fast track corporate climber, pretty boy, family man. His "apprentice" is Miles, the Intern. Miles is as fresh as they come right out of design school which makes him so endearing. His naivety and innocence may eventually be eroded by the real world but his spirit is galvanized by the refreshing creed that architecture can, and will, make the world a better place.

Every firm has an "old man" that can run rings around any underling when it comes to putting a building together. The old timer at Dezinefirm Inc is Jerry. The tragedy is that he would rather gouge out his eye with a protractor than to right-click a mouse. He is tortured by the political games of the office that have slowly evolved around him. It is his own personal integrity that made him choose not to play.

The supporting cast includes Chuck the Contractor; Dezinefirm's foil and chronically low bidder. Tom is the design school student. He will graduate, one day, but why? Architecture was so pure in school so why not just suspend that simple time ? His authoritarian mentor is Professor Walker, the predominant academic figure. Walker is a man of mystery. We are not aware of his true talent or his personal life, only his steadfast love for his work.

ARCH TV is the 24 hour a day television channel for all things related to architecture. It is owned by Doug, a community access channel robber baron that has spearheaded groundbreaking architectural game shows and live design award coverage. The station's protagonist is Wyatt, the emcee and number one fan fave that hosts memorable architecture episodes such as Archi-Music Countdown.

There are also a variety of fantasy panels interlaced throughout this compendium. For example, The Architect's Dream Sequence series are depictions of the daydreams that we professionals would like our world to be, or in some cases, are scared to death that it could be. Forgotten Movements in Architecture is my way of just having fun with all of the "isms" and labels that seem so necessary for critics to pronounce, yet so shallow when discussing the true depth and soul of architecture.

I know that *Archi-toons* will bring a smile to your face and a thought to your mind. I love what I do but I also need to get some billable time in for this month so I need to go. There will be more Archi-toons to come because I can't stop them if I tried. Please feel free to visit the Archi-toons family at www.archi-toons.com or drop me an email and tell me what you think.

Richard T. Bynum, Jr.
April 2003

ABOUT THE AUTHOR

Richard T. Bynum, Jr., AIA is the founder and principal of Bynum Architecture in Greenville, SC. Prior to forming Bynum Architecture in 1996, the author worked with several of the Southeast's most prestigious architectural firms. These included Thompson, Ventulett, Stainback and Associates in Atlanta, GA; Walter Robbs Callahan and Pierce in Winston-Salem, NC; LS3P in Charleston, SC and Lamar T. Webb in St. Simons Island, GA. Mr. Bynum has a Master of Architecture Degree from Clemson University in Clemson, SC and a Bachelor of Environmental Design in Architecture from North Carolina State University in Raleigh, NC. He is an active member of the American Institute of Architects and has authored over 20 articles on various topics for AIA publications. His first book, *The Handbokk of Alternative Materials in Residential Construction*, was written with Daniel L. Rubino and published by McGraw Hill Professional Book Group in 1998. His second book, *The Architect's Planner 2000*, was published by McGraw Hill Professional Book Group in 1999. His third book, *The Handbook of Residential Insulation* was published by McGraw Hill Professional Book Group in 2000.

Richard T. Bynum, Jr.
April 2003

Banned Sand

Evolution of an Architectural Firm

Have it Your Way

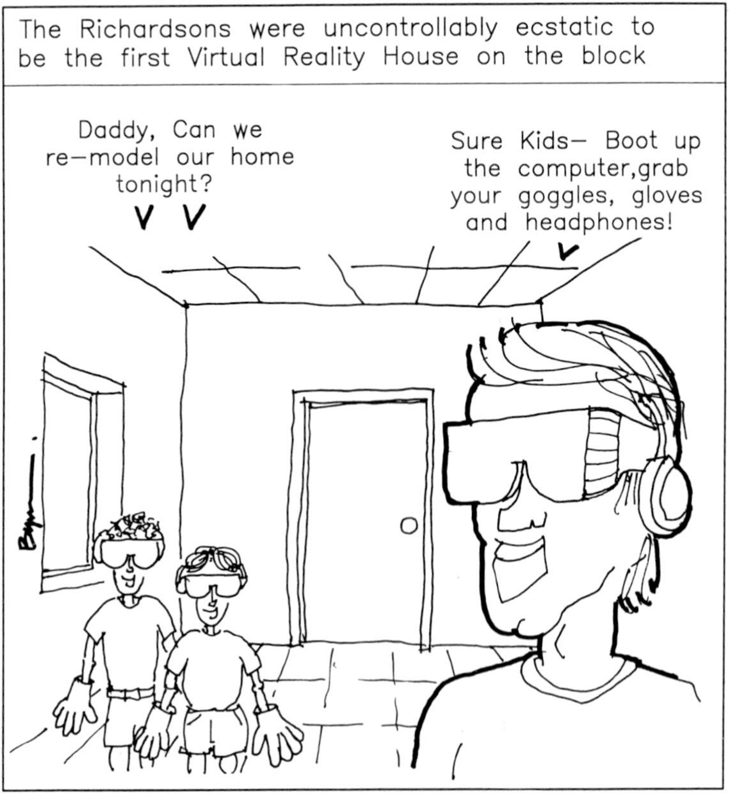

Virtual Reality

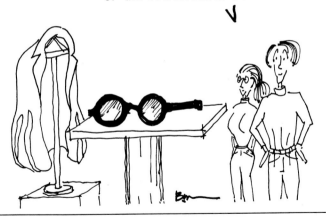

Fashion Statement

Impressionable Youth

Architectural Mathematics 101

The Venturi Effect

Judgement Day

Guerilla Marketing

Fresh out of college, Miles the intern suddenly felt like a kid in a candy store
...and this is the office supply room...
WOW ! Look at all of that bumwad, post-its, markers, prismas, sharpies, tape dots.....and it's all free!!!

The Perk

Architect's Dream Sequence # 17

Arch TV, the fledgling, 24 hour Architecture Channel, struggled with quality programming....

Design is his Mistress

Rite of Passage

Start 'em Young

Count Rumford would be Proud

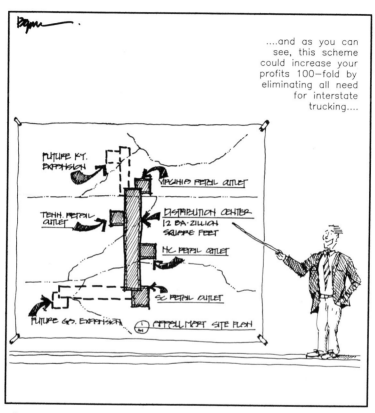

"Appall-Mart" reviews plans for a new Southeastern Distribution Center....

A rare glimpse into the competitive
world of an architectural intern's Agent

Low gas prices, low mortgage rates and expanding suburban developments provided the perfect environment for a dramatic shift in architectural design...

Forgotten Movements in Architecture:
"Commuterism"

Stress Relief Kit for
all Do-It-Yourselfers

The NFL's undeniable impact
on Architectural Interns...

Convoluted Continuing Ed

Even Arch TV Succumbed to the
Seductive Power of the Game Show...

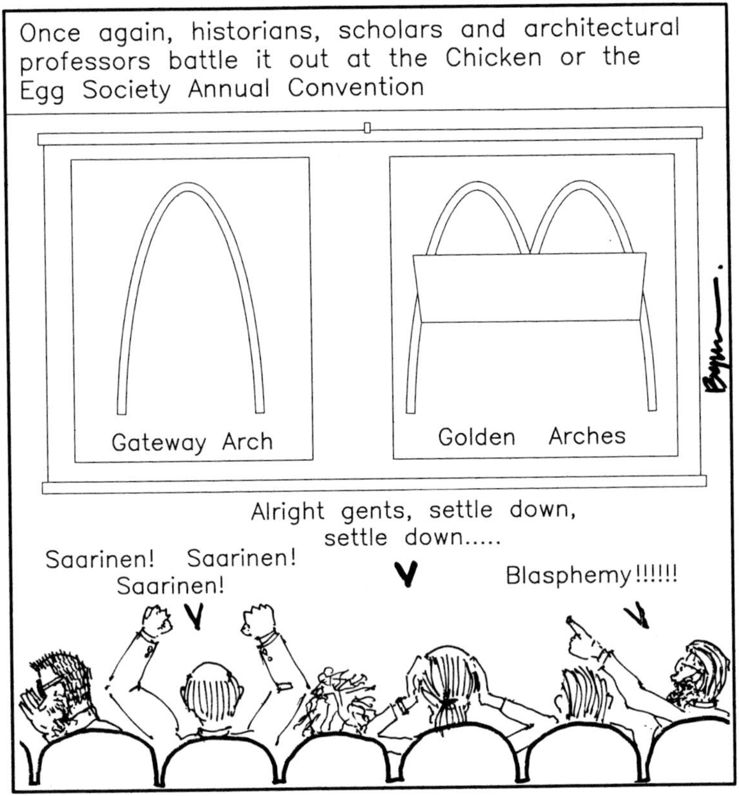

Which Came First ?

Architectural Eyesore Disposal?

The Cherry Tree Chronicles

35

Back to you in the Studio, Steve

Metricks

The Family Gaudí at the beach ...

Mocked by many, Walter Gropius's faithful dog, Otto, had design aspirations of his own......

The Woof-bund

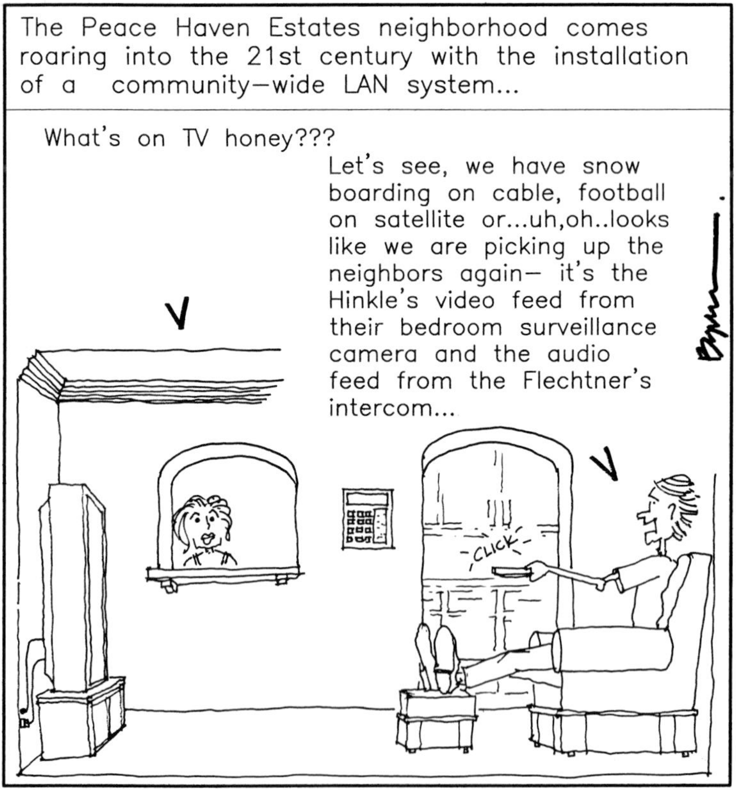

The Not-So-Smart Home...

The first glimpse that ~~America's~~ the World's Greatest architect, Frank Lloyd Wright, may have possessed a modest streak of vanity......

DEAR FLW,

I LOVE ME

LOVE, FLW

Happy Valentine's Day

Lost in Space Planning

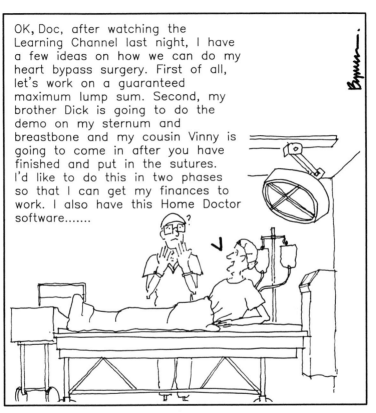

Be it Architecture or Medicine, some Clients are all the same.......

Arch TV, beseiged by low ratings, ventured into the wacky world of music television...

Starchitect Scribbles

'Cause it's our Cause

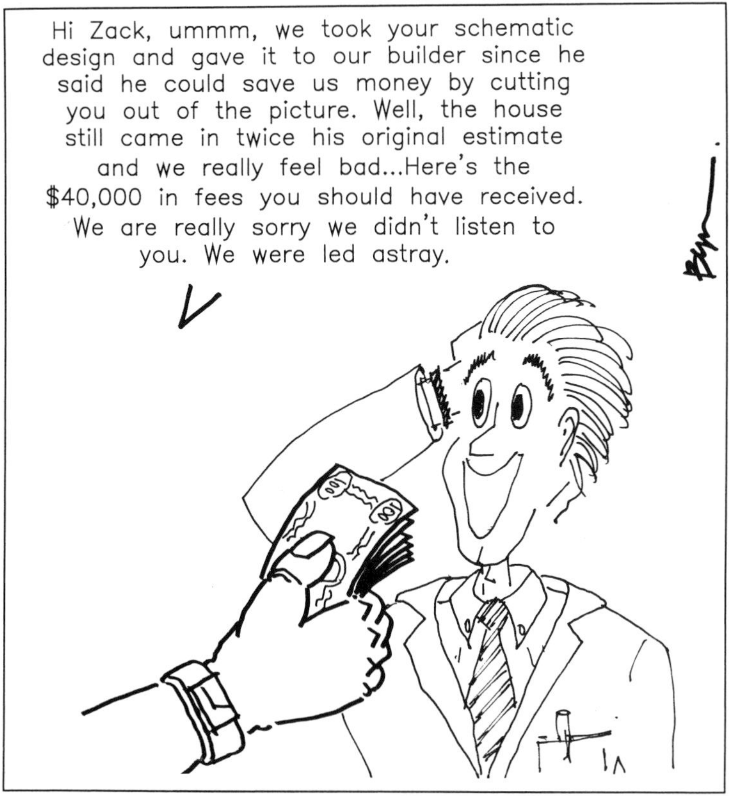

Architect's Dream Sequence # 44

New discoveries in plant grafting opened the floral market to a revolutionary breed of celebrity architect—inspired horticultural delights.

WRIGHTENIA

MACKINTOSHA

HORTASIA

Designer Flowers

Caddiction

Upon full restoration of the original 1783 artwork, Etienne—Louis Boullee's sketches revealed additional details not previously known about Newton's Cenotaph.....

Design for a Bowling Alley

Arch TV's spin-off, Archi-music television
was running low on material after two shows....

Growing Pains

Time Bumb

A Shop Drawing is worth
a Thousand Words

Scale Shock

Forgotten Movements in Architecture:
"Distortionism"

Even in the 23rd Century, crafty homeowners can still find loopholes in the most stringent of Neighborhood Design Covenants.

Log Cabin Revivalism?

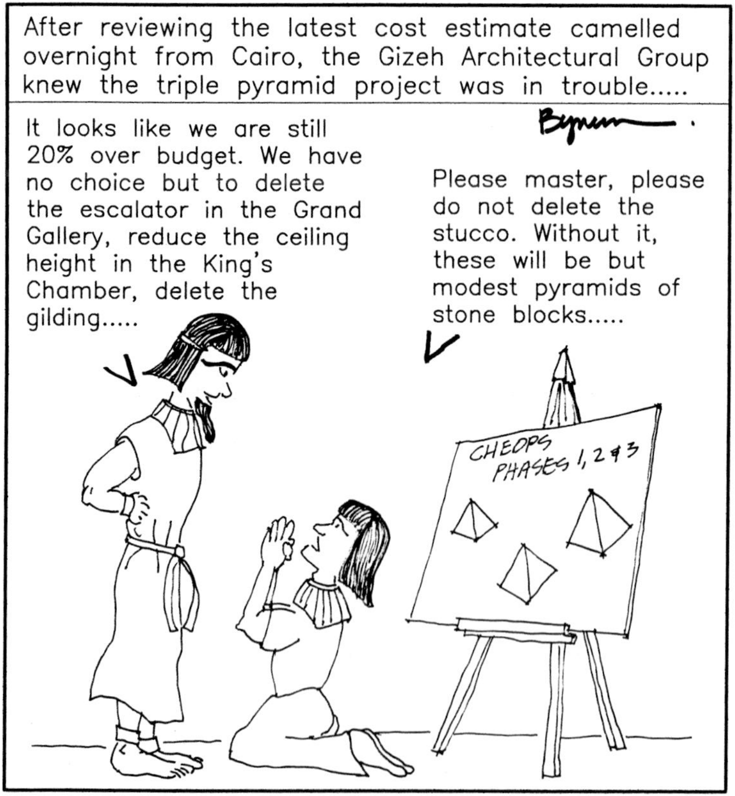

Value Engineering, The Early Years

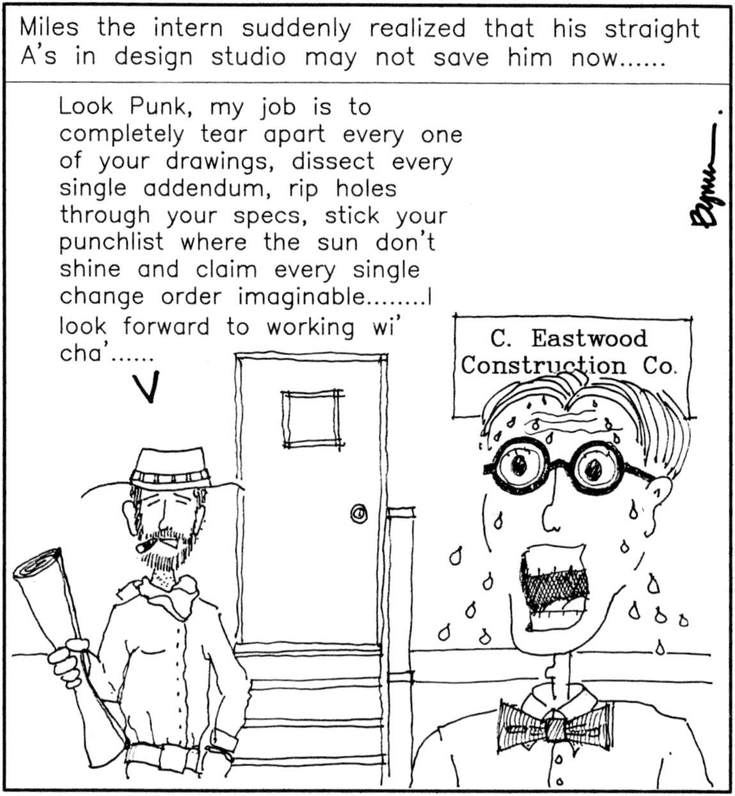

CA Initiation

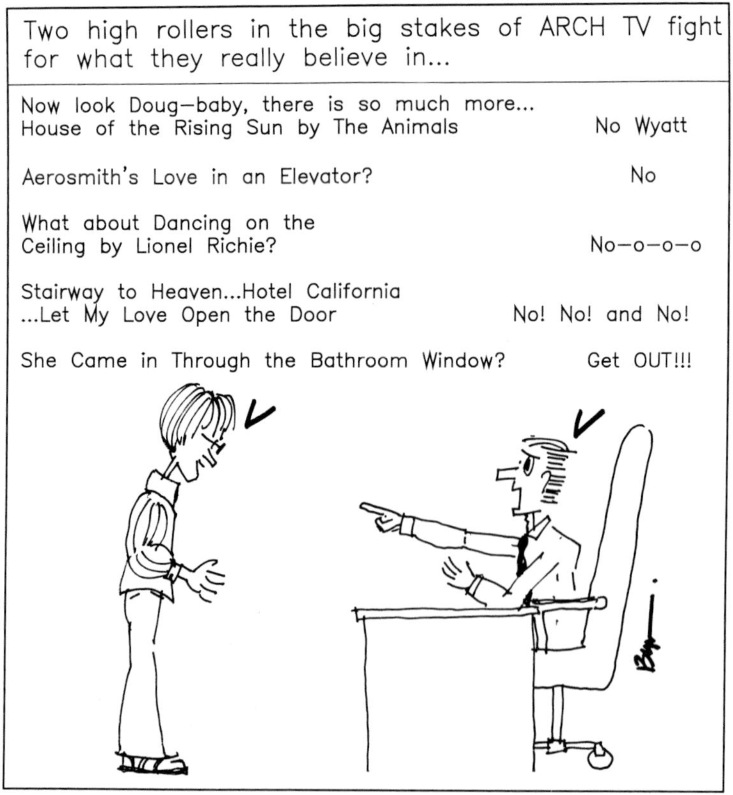

Behind the scenes at Archi-music Television's rapid demise

The Magic Wand

Imagery Run Amuck

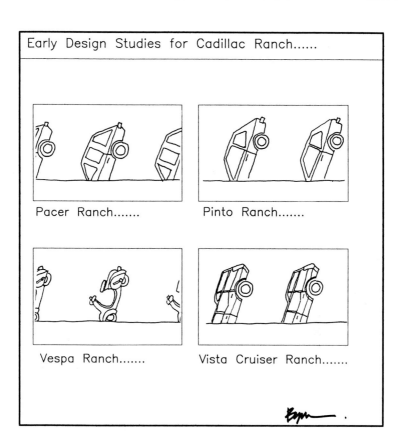

If at First You Don't Succeed.....

Living Vicariously?

Forgotten Movements in Architecture:
"Botulism"

Dear Diary

Miles the intern was not sure whether he was going to find the annual Eisenmann Office summer picnic.

To Peter's House:
Follow the flight path of the Philadelphia/New York Shuttle for 3.7 miles, turn left at the 3rd stoplight beyond the exploited subway tunnel that is collinear with the Aries and Big Dipper constellations, go for 2 miles past the baseball park and follow the abstracted axis created when connecting the left field and right field light towers. Turn left at House XX, right at House VI and left at House IX. Look for red staircase.

(Metric version available upon request)

Deconstructivist Directions

Arch TV: Blues Night

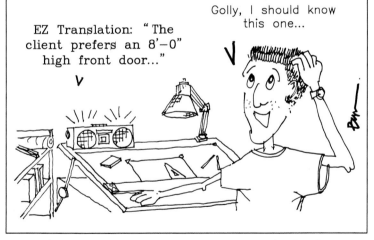

Tom the freshman was enamored with Professor Walker's "Design Studio-EZ" Language Tapes.

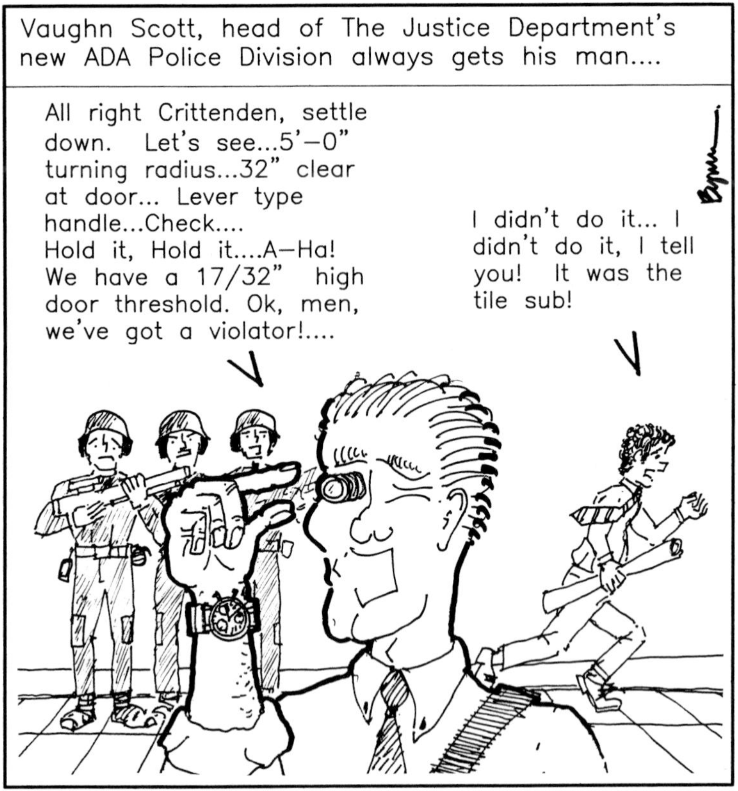

Accessible or Excessible

Mannerism meets Mick......

Window
Zuccari, Rome
c. 1590

Mouth
Jagger, Rolling Stones
c. 1971

Elite Culture vs Pop Culture

Recessions Do Breed Character

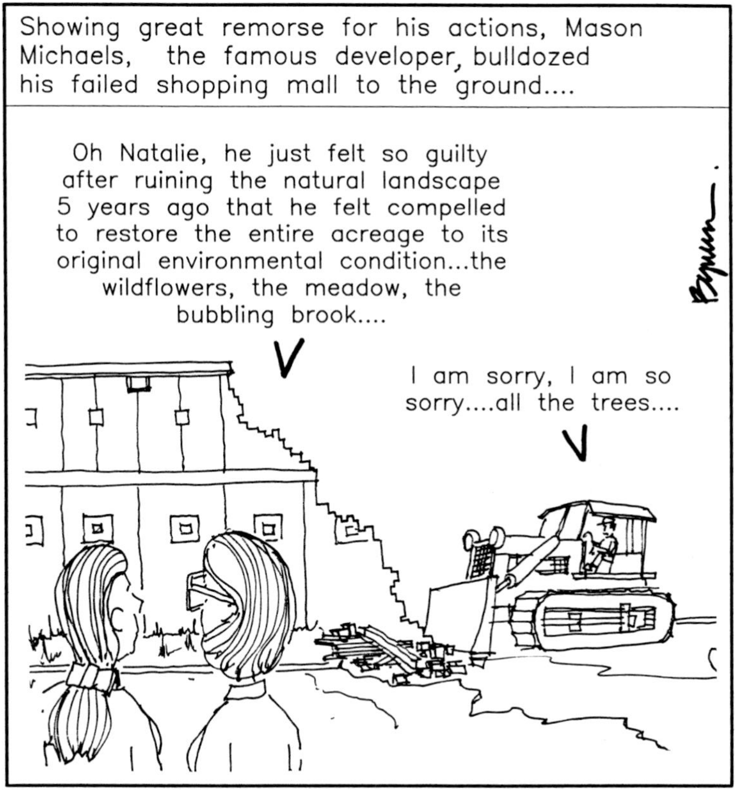

Architect's Dream Sequence # 31

The Tudor Style was never the same after the four lovable mop—tops arrived in the States.....

Forgotten Movements in Architecture:
"Beatle-ism"

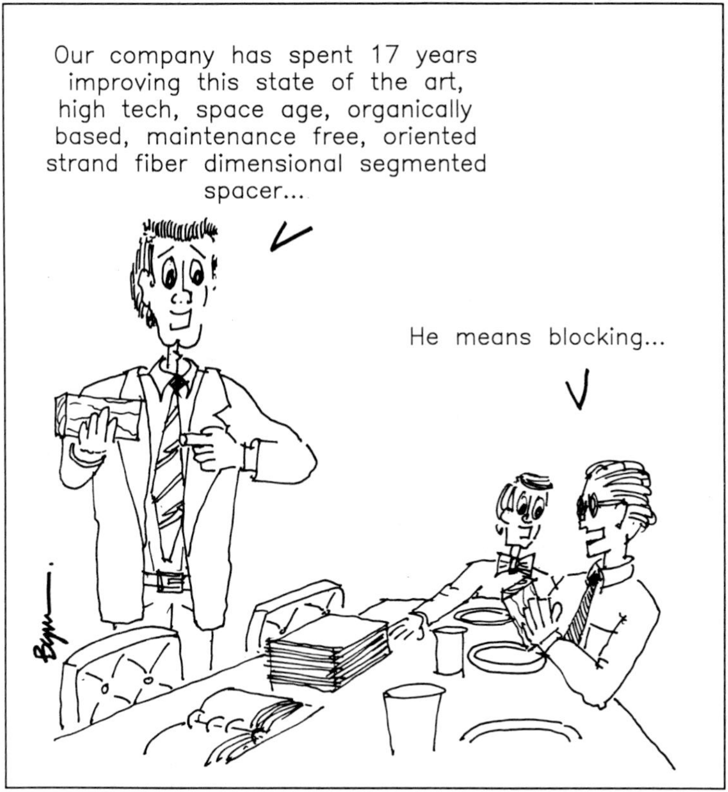

It's All in the Presentation

The Bauhaus's brief experiment
with corporate sponsorship.....

Batty Clients

Arch TV Goes Reality Show

Actions Speak Louder than Words

Endpoint, Intersection, Node.......

CAD Mad

Quick & Easy Cost Estimating

A rare glimpse into the world of Cro—Magnon Hunters & Gatherers.....

Grogg— You call yourself a Cave designer? Megaraptors and Suns are old hat. Wilma told me that Woolly Mammoths are in this year!

A Man's Home is His Cave

Spec Writer's Lament

July 4th, The Rest of the Story

Miller mysteriously found himself in a strange place— Architectural Photography—Land!

It is s—o—o—o beautiful and ordered...but wait.....There are no Alarm Clocks.....There are no Telephones.....That flower arrangement is in three places at the same time......

Architect's Dream Sequence # 61

The growing number of home-based businesses in the 1990's helped spawn a rare, suburban-based psychosis known as "skyscraper-envy."

Forgotten Movements in Architecture:
"Towerism"

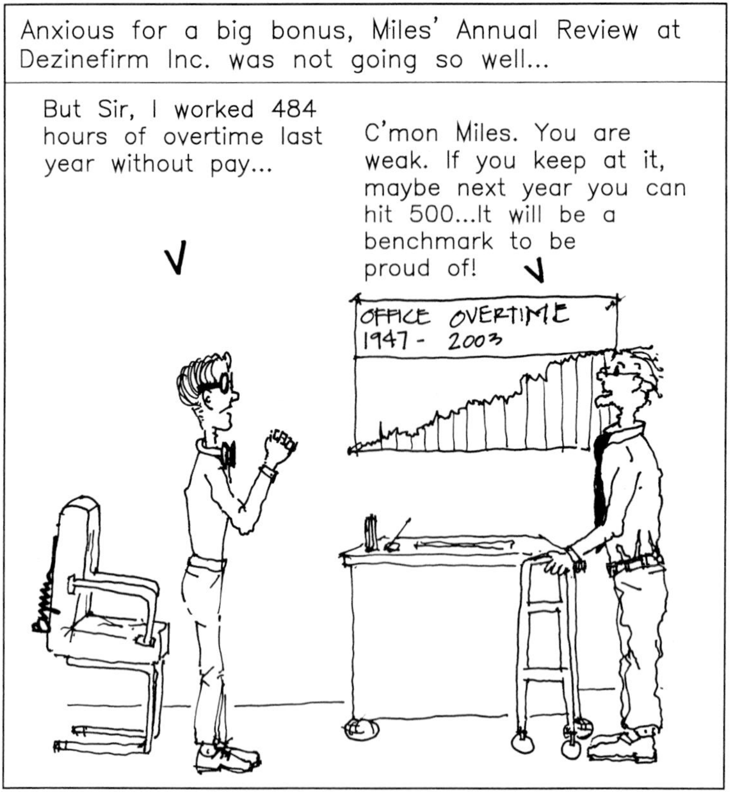

Administration Gap, Generation Gap

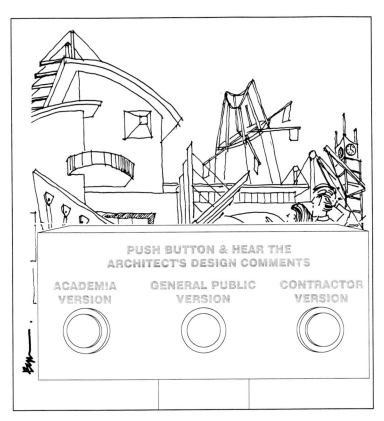

WHAT DOES IT ALL MEAN?

The First Annual Design Symposium of
TV Architects and Interior Designers.....

Glass House Architects
throwing stones.........

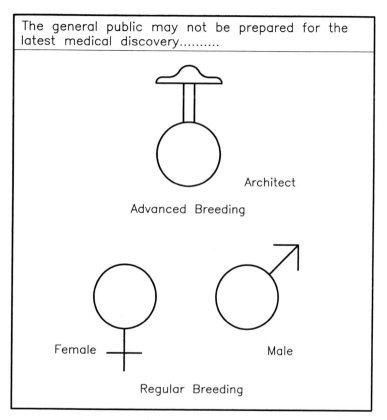

The general public may not be prepared for the latest medical discovery..........

Architect

Advanced Breeding

Female

Male

Regular Breeding

Biology's dirty little secret..........

Architect's Dream Sequence # 62

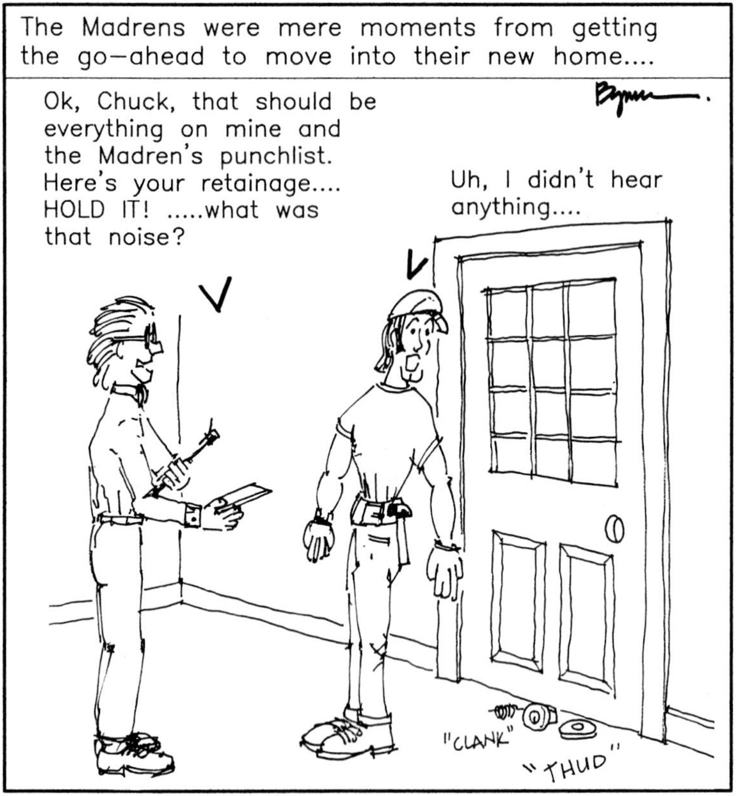

Timing is Everything

Child's Play

Assimilation is Futile

Inspired by the immensely popular Beatle & Star Trek Conventions, promoters were shocked at the success of the latest cult—like fan gathering, the "This Old House" Convention......

MEET STEVE'S 2ND COUSIN—BALLROOM A

THEME MUSIC ON CD !!

GLUE—ON BEARDS

VINTAGE VILA STUFF

USED NAILS FROM THE SHOW HERE

FLANNEL SHIRTS JUST LIKE NORM'S !

Imitation or Flattery

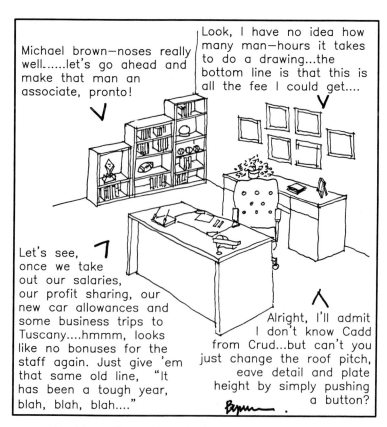

If the Boss's Walls Could Talk

Smorgas-bored

The Cartoonland Design Awards

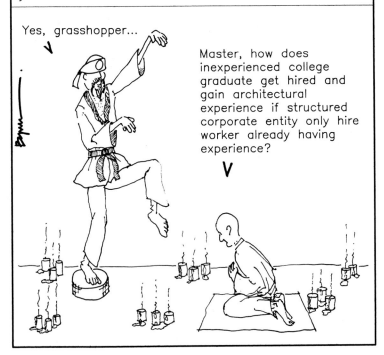

Kung Fu, the lost episodes.....

Beasley Architectural Development reveals the name of the mega—developer's newest project at the ceremonial groundbreaking...

Ladies, and Gentlemen, I am pleased to announce that the B.A.D. marketing department, after years of research, have created the signage that will undeniably enhance the image of this development... and prove that architectural aesthetics, style and quality are secondary to a good office park name!

Shangri—La Stoney Brook
Greenbriar River View
Wood Ridge Park Valley
Dale Falls Office Park

What's in a Name?

Makin' It Look Easy

Happy Thanksgiving

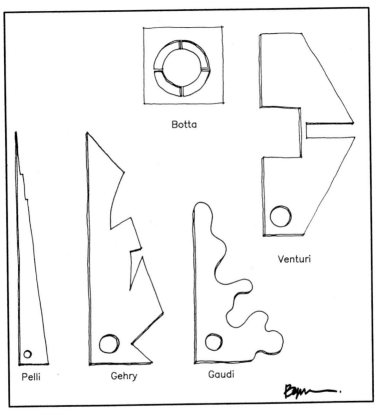

Botta

Venturi

Pelli

Gehry

Gaudi

Triangles and Templates of the Stars

Extremist Corporate Team Building

"Draw Your Dream-House Day" in
Mrs. Mackie's kindergarten class

AIA Commandos bust up another
Learning Unit Swapping Ring

Archi-tether

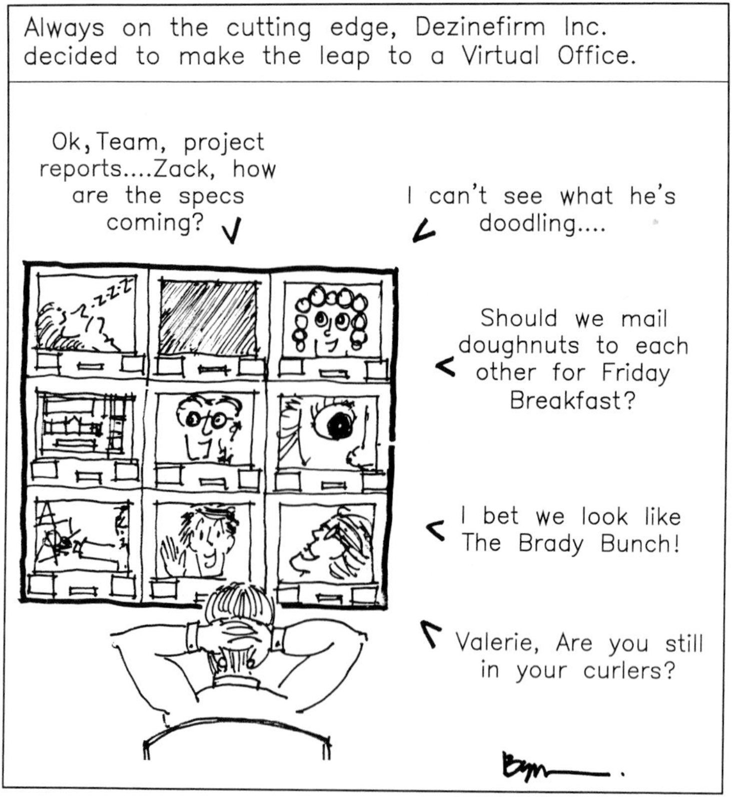

Virtual Nightmare

Another Argument against Television
in the Classroom

It became apparent at the pre-bid conference that Dezinefirm's transition to Con–Doc Keynoting may be frustrating for some individuals.

Confound-Doc

Code-elepsy

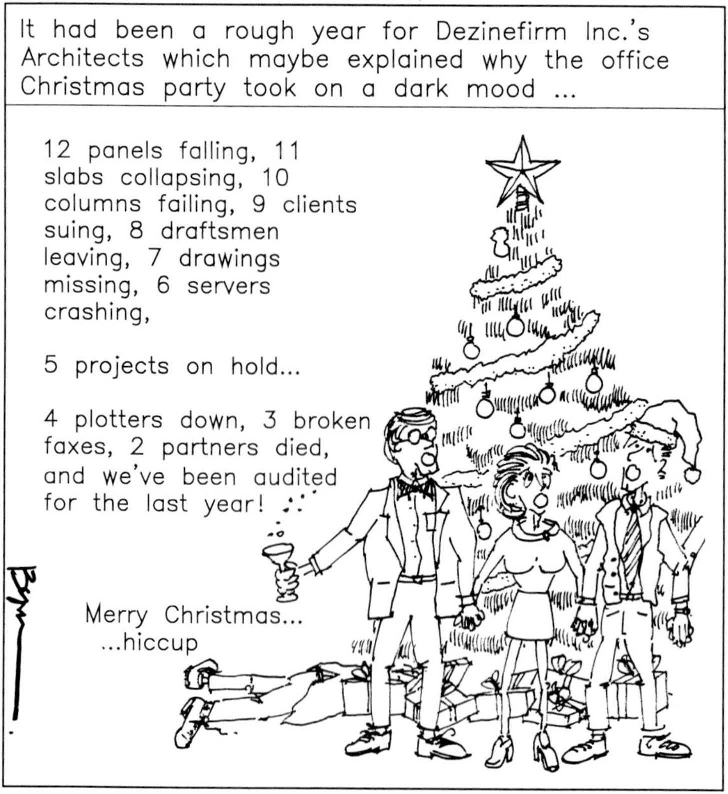

It had been a rough year for Dezinefirm Inc.'s Architects which maybe explained why the office Christmas party took on a dark mood ...

12 panels falling, 11 slabs collapsing, 10 columns failing, 9 clients suing, 8 draftsmen leaving, 7 drawings missing, 6 servers crashing,

5 projects on hold...

4 plotters down, 3 broken faxes, 2 partners died, and we've been audited for the last year!

Merry Christmas...
...hiccup

Holiday Jeer

Star Architect Training Camp

23rd Century Froebel Blocks

1-900-BAD-DESIGN, Call Me, Now

Guggencycle

Compass Anybody?

Klimt Family Picnic, Vienna, 1908